STUDY GUIDES

Science

Year 3

Alan Jarvis and
William Merrick

RISING STARS

Rising Stars UK Ltd, 22 Grafton Street, London W1S 4EX

www.risingstars-uk.com

Published 2007

Reprinted 2008

Text, design and layout © Rising Stars UK Ltd.

Design: HL Studios and Clive Sutherland

Illustrations: Bookmatrix (Beehive Illustrations)

Editorial project management: Dodi Beardshaw

Editorial: Marieke O'Connor

Cover design: Burville-Riley Partnership

British Library Cataloguing in Publication Data.

A CIP record for this book is available from the British Library.

ISBN: 978-1-84680-094-8

Printed by: Craft Print International Limited, Singapore

Contents

How to get the best out of this book

Each topic spreads across two pages and focuses on one major idea. Many of your lessons may be based on these topics. Each double page helps you to keep **On track** and **Aiming higher**.

Title and key ideas: tell you what you are aiming to learn. The second idea is always more difficult than the first.

Key information: sets out the key facts that you need to know and the ideas you need to understand fully.

Key questions: help you to learn more facts and understand the science in each topic. The investigations you do will give you the evidence you need to prove the scientific facts you've learnt.

Key words and their meanings: help build up your scientific vocabulary. Remember that some words mean one thing in everyday life and something more special in science.

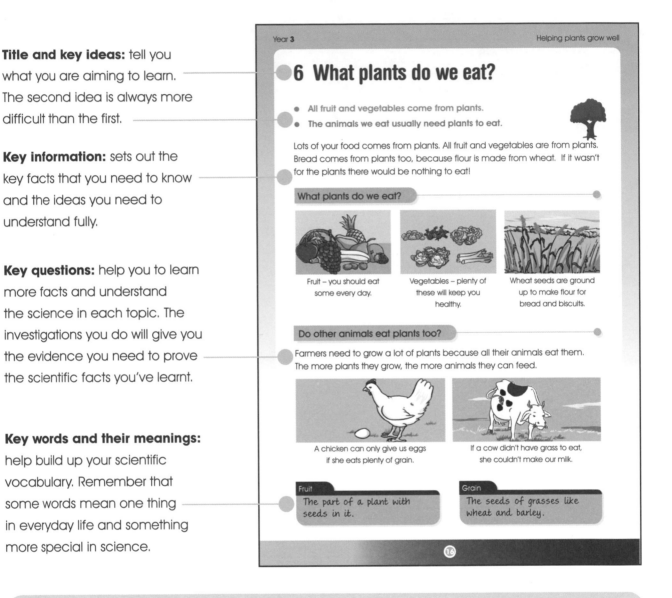

Year **3**

Helping plants grow well

6 What plants do we eat?

- All fruit and vegetables come from plants.
- The animals we eat usually need plants to eat.

Lots of your food comes from plants. All fruit and vegetables are from plants. Bread comes from plants too, because flour is made from wheat. If it wasn't for the plants there would be nothing to eat!

What plants do we eat?

Fruit – you should eat some every day.

Vegetables – plenty of these will keep you healthy.

Wheat seeds are ground up to make flour for bread and biscuits.

Do other animals eat plants too?

Farmers need to grow a lot of plants because all their animals eat them. The more plants they grow, the more animals they can feed.

A chicken can only give us eggs if she eats plenty of grain.

If a cow didn't have grass to eat, she couldn't make our milk.

Fruit
The part of a plant with seeds in it.

Grain
The seeds of grasses like wheat and barley.

16

Follow these simple rules if you are using the book for revising.

1 Read each page carefully. Give yourself time to take in each idea.

2 Learn the key facts and ideas. Ask your teacher or mum, dad or the adult who looks after you if you need help.

3 Concentrate on the things you find more difficult.

4 Only work for about 20 minutes or so at a time. Take a break and then do more work.

The right-hand page has lots of fun questions for you to try. They are like the National Curriculum test questions you will do. The answers are in the pull-out section in the middle of this book.

If you get most of the **On track** questions right, then you know you are working at level 3. Well done – that's brilliant! If you get most of the **Aiming higher** questions right, you are working at the higher level 4. You're really doing well!

Helping plants grow well   6 What plants do we eat?

Test your learning

On track

1   Jack is out shopping for fruit and vegetables. There are so many different ones to choose from! He decides to make two lists of their names, one for fruit and one for vegetables.

(a) Finish off these lists. Try to put ten different things in each list.

Fruit	Vegetables
oranges	cabbage
apples	potatoes

(b) Wheat is the name of the seeds of a special sort of grass that farmers grow. What foods in the supermarket are made from wheat?

Aiming higher

2   Jack's mum tells him that most of the animals on the farm eat plants. Copy the table. Match up these farm animals with the food they like to eat.

sheep ducks
chickens rabbits

(a)

Animal	What plant does it eat?
	mixed grains
	carrots
	pondweed
	grass

(b) Farmer Brown's farm sends plenty of milk to the supermarket. Why does Farmer Brown need to grow a lot of grass on his farm?

How well am I doing?

On track	Aiming higher
I can write a list of five plants that people eat.	I can say what plants some farm animals eat.

⑰

SAT-style questions: help you to find out how well you have understood what you have learnt. There are questions on facts, ideas and scientific investigations. If you are stuck, the information on the left-hand page will help. **Write all your answers in your notebook.**

On track questions: come in different styles. Be sure to read each one carefully. Think about what the diagrams are telling you.

Aiming higher questions: are more difficult. To answer them well, you have to know more facts or understand a harder idea.

How well am I doing?: helps you to find out the level you are working at. Keep a running record of how well you are doing so you keep on target.

Follow these simple rules if you want to know how well you are doing.

1 Work through the questions.

2 Keep a record of how well you do.

3 If you are working at level 3 you will get most of the **On track** questions correct.

4 If you are working at level 4 you will also get most of the **Aiming higher** questions correct.

1 What types of food are there?

- Food can be put into a few main groups.

- **Some food groups help us to grow and some give us energy.**

Count up how many types of food you eat in a week. There are so many different ones! To make it easy to learn about them we can put them into **food groups**. Each type is good for us in different ways.

What are the main food groups?

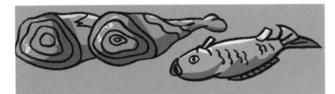

meat and fish

fats and oils

sugar and starch

fruit and vegetables

What are different foods for?

Foods for growth

Meat and fish help us to grow and build our muscles. So do milk, cheese, eggs and pulses.

Grow

To get bigger.

Foods for energy

Bread, rice, pasta, potatoes and sugar give us the energy we need to keep active.

Energy

What we use up when we run around. We get it from food.

Test your learning

On track

1   Here are some foods from Yin's kitchen.

         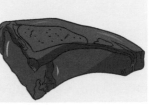

cake   olive oil   tomato   lamb chop

(a) Copy this table. Use it to match up the name of each food
with the food types.

fruits and vegetables	tomato
meat and fish	
fats and oils	
sugars and starches	

(b) Yin had some bread and butter. What were the two main types of food
she was eating?

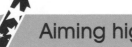

Aiming higher

2   Yin is growing up fast. She is 5 cm taller than she was last year!

(a) From this list, pick three foods that will help build her muscles.

> sugar   eggs   chocolate   cheese   meat   oranges

(b) What foods should we eat to give us energy to run and keep warm?

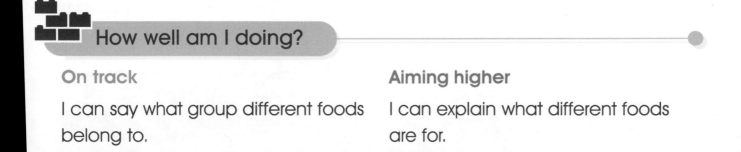

How well am I doing?

On track

I can say what group different foods
belong to.

Aiming higher

I can explain what different foods
are for.

2 How can eating keep you healthy?

- You must eat the right amount – not too much and not too little.
- Different foods keep you healthy in different ways.

Have you ever eaten too much and given yourself a tummy ache? Have you ever left your dinner because you didn't like it? Always try to eat the right amount, and have a good mixture of different foods every day.

How much should you eat?

If you keep on eating too much you could get too fat. It will slow you down.

If you don't eat enough you will be thin, and be too tired to do anything.

What is best to eat?

You need to eat some of each **food type** every day. Your diet should be as **varied** as possible. Then your diet will be **balanced** and you will be healthy.

This is a good meal. The chicken builds up your muscles, the potatoes and butter give you energy, and the vegetables keep you healthy.

This is not as good. There is too much fat and not enough vegetables. Too much of this will make you ill.

Diet

The mixture of different foods you eat each day.

Balanced diet

A diet with the right amount of each type of food.

Test your learning

On track

1 Efik's dad is getting too fat! He is much bigger than he was. He does
   not fit into his old clothes. He also walks slower than he used to.
   Here are some things he could do:

   - He could buy some bigger clothes.
   - He could eat less.
   - He could take more rest.
   - He could take more exercise.

(a) Which would help him lose weight?

(b) If he could lose weight, what would be the main thing to show
    that he was healthier?

   - He could keep his old clothes.   • He could walk faster.
   - He would look thinner.   • He could eat more food.

Aiming higher

2 Efik wants to be healthy. He has heard that he
   needs to eat a balanced diet.

(a) Which one of these pieces of advice will help him
    to eat a balanced diet?

   - Never eat sweets.   • Eat lots of different foods.
   - Don't eat too much.   • Eat only vegetables.

(b) Efik's favourite meal is chicken and chips. What else should he
    have with it to make it healthier?

How well am I doing?

On track

I know why I need to eat just the right
amount of food.

Aiming higher

I can explain why I need many
different types of food to stay healthy.

3 What do animals eat?

- Different animals eat different foods.
- **Animals have special teeth for their different foods.**

Have you ever noticed that different pets like different foods?
A rabbit will nibble grass but a cat leaves it alone. A cat likes meat
or fish better than grass. The animals know what's best for them.

What do different pets eat?

Mrs Novak's class wrote down what their pets liked to eat. They noticed that
some animals live on meat, and others live on plants.

	Food from animals		Food from plants	
	meat	fish	grass	seeds
cats	3	2		
dogs	5			
rabbits			3	
mice				2

We give cats and dogs tinned food but they are actually
hunters. They catch other animals (like rabbits and mice)
and eat them. Rabbits and mice eat plants.

Do pets have special teeth to eat their favourite foods?

Cats and dogs have long sharp fangs to
catch animals when they are hunting and
to tear off meat. Fangs are called
canine teeth.

The sharp front teeth of a rabbit are good
at cutting grass. They are called
incisor teeth.

Canine tooth

A tooth for tearing; sometimes
we call them fangs.

Incisor tooth

A tooth for cutting or
nibbling.

Test your learning

On track

1   Panther class made a table about what their pets eat.

	Food from animals	Food from plants
	meat and fish	grass or seeds
cats	5	0
dogs	5	0
rabbits	0	3
mice	0	2

(a) Show the results on bar charts like these.

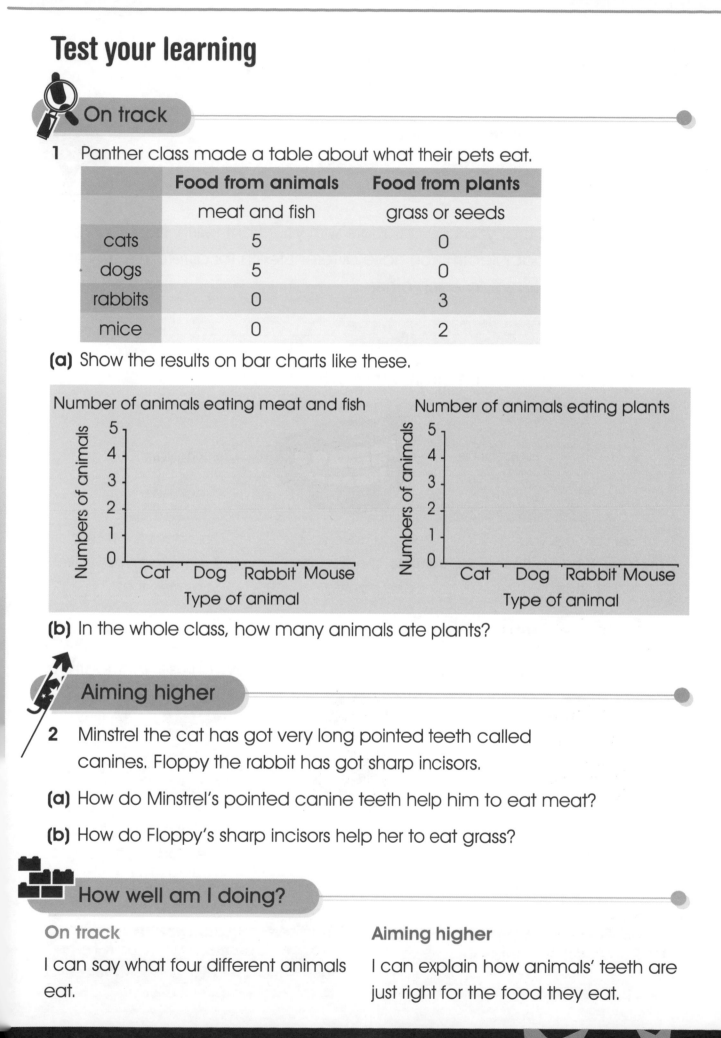

(b) In the whole class, how many animals ate plants?

Aiming higher

2   Minstrel the cat has got very long pointed teeth called canines. Floppy the rabbit has got sharp incisors.

(a) How do Minstrel's pointed canine teeth help him to eat meat?

(b) How do Floppy's sharp incisors help her to eat grass?

How well am I doing?

On track

I can say what four different animals eat.

Aiming higher

I can explain how animals' teeth are just right for the food they eat.

4 What teeth have you got?

- Humans have different types of teeth.
- The different types of teeth do different jobs for us while we eat.

Have you noticed that you bite an apple with your front teeth, but then you chew it with your back teeth? You have different teeth for different jobs. Let's see if they look different to each other.

What kinds of teeth do you have?

You can look at your own teeth in a mirror.

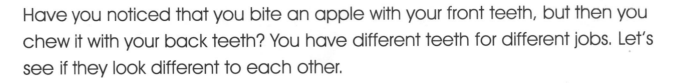

incisors — molars — canines

At the front are your **incisors**. They are flat and sharp.

Next you have your **canines**. They are long and pointed.

Your back teeth are called **molars**. They have wide tops.

What are the different teeth for?

Next time you eat a meal you can think about the way you use your teeth.

Your sharp front teeth work like scissors to cut off pieces of food.

You can use your pointy canines to tear off something tough like meat.

Your flat molars grind up the food so you can swallow it.

Grind

To mash up something.

Swallow

To send something down from your mouth into your stomach.

Test your learning

On track

1 Lucy looked at the teeth in her mouth.

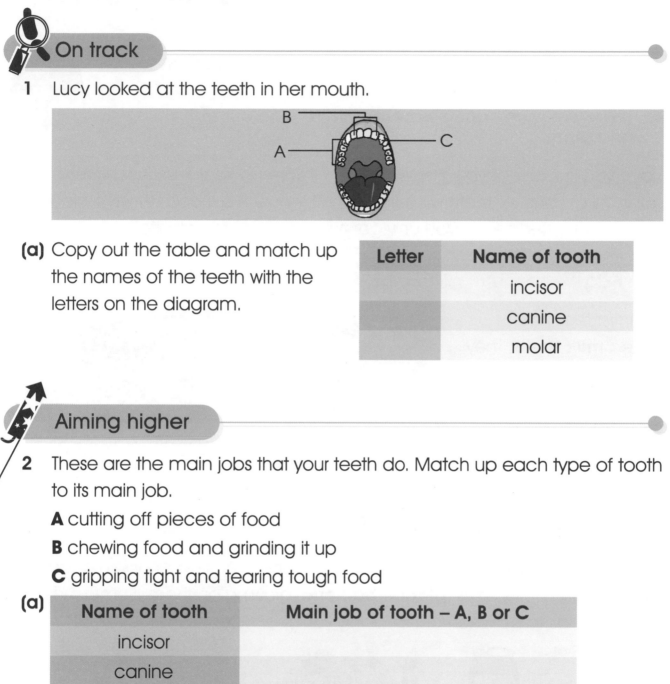

(a) Copy out the table and match up the names of the teeth with the letters on the diagram.

Letter	Name of tooth
	incisor
	canine
	molar

Aiming higher

2 These are the main jobs that your teeth do. Match up each type of tooth to its main job.

A cutting off pieces of food

B chewing food and grinding it up

C gripping tight and tearing tough food

(a)

Name of tooth	Main job of tooth – A, B or C
incisor	
canine	
molar	

(b) Explain how the shape of an incisor tooth helps it to do its job.

How well am I doing?

On track

I can name the three different kinds of teeth.

Aiming higher

I can explain what job each kind of tooth does.

5 How can you look after your teeth?

- Humans only get two sets of teeth. Our second set has to last forever!
- There are many good ways of looking after our teeth and gums.

Have you lost any of your first teeth yet? Children in Year 3 usually have a few gaps. All of your first teeth will fall out one by one. A second set will replace them. Look after them – you only get two sets in your whole life!

Why do we lose our milk teeth?

Your first teeth are called **milk teeth**. They are just right for your small mouth. When you grow up, you will need bigger teeth.

It isn't a problem when a child loses a milk tooth. New ones soon grow.

If a grown-up loses a tooth, it's a big shame. The gap will be there forever!

How can we look after our teeth?

Teeth can go bad and can give you toothache. This is called tooth decay and is caused by germs (**plaque bacteria**) growing on them. Sometimes the tooth has to be taken out. Brushing your teeth cleans the germs off.

Sweets and sugary drinks will feed the germs that rot teeth.

Carrots and apples are better for your teeth because they have less sugar. They don't feed the germs.

Brushing your teeth before you go to bed keeps them safe all night.

Milk teeth
Your first set of teeth.

Decay
Anything rotting is decaying.

Test your learning

 On track

1   Cecilia is seven years old. One of her front teeth has fallen out! Her mum says not to worry, as one will soon grow to take its place.

(a) What is the name given to your first set of teeth?

(b) How many sets of teeth will Cecilia have altogether?

(c) Why do you need to replace your first teeth?

Aiming higher

2   Cecilia has made a list of good ideas to help Panther class look after their teeth. Her first idea was:

> Brush your teeth twice a day.

(a) Write down two more rules she can put in her list.

(b) Explain why brushing your teeth makes them last longer.

How well am I doing?

On track	Aiming higher
I know how many sets of teeth I will have when I grow up.	I know how to look after my teeth.

6 What plants do we eat?

- All fruit and vegetables come from plants.
- The animals we eat usually need plants to eat.

Lots of your food comes from plants. All fruit and vegetables are from plants. Bread comes from plants too, because flour is made from wheat. If it wasn't for the plants there would be nothing to eat!

What plants do we eat?

Fruit – you should eat some every day.

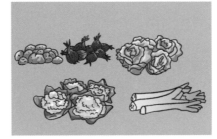

Vegetables – plenty of these will keep you healthy.

Wheat seeds are ground up to make flour for bread and biscuits.

Do other animals eat plants too?

Farmers need to grow a lot of plants because all their animals eat them. The more plants they grow, the more animals they can feed.

A chicken can only give us eggs if she eats plenty of grain.

If a cow didn't have grass to eat, she couldn't make our milk.

Fruit

The part of a plant with seeds in it.

Grain

The seeds of grasses like wheat and barley.

Test your learning

On track

1 Jack is out shopping for fruit and vegetables. There are so many different ones to choose from! He decides to make two lists of their names, one for fruit and one for vegetables.

(a) Finish off these lists. Try to put ten different things in each list.

Fruit	Vegetables
oranges apples	cabbage potatoes

(b) Wheat is the name of the seeds of a special sort of grass that farmers grow. What foods in the supermarket are made from wheat?

Aiming higher

2 Jack's mum tells him that most of the animals on the farm eat plants. Copy the table. Match up these farm animals with the food they like to eat.

sheep   ducks
chickens   rabbits

(a)

Animal	What plant does it eat?
	mixed grains
	carrots
	pondweed
	grass

(b) Farmer Brown's farm sends plenty of milk to the supermarket. Why does Farmer Brown need to grow a lot of grass on his farm?

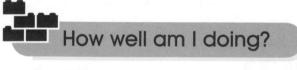

How well am I doing?

On track

I can write a list of five plants that people eat.

Aiming higher

I can say what plants some farm animals eat.

7 How fast do plants grow?

- You can measure a plant's length with a ruler as it grows.
- To get a good idea of how plants grow, you need to measure a few.

The grass in your garden looks long after about two weeks in the summer. If you sit and watch a plant it doesn't seem to grow at all, but if you measure it every day you will soon see a difference.

Can you measure a plant as it grows?

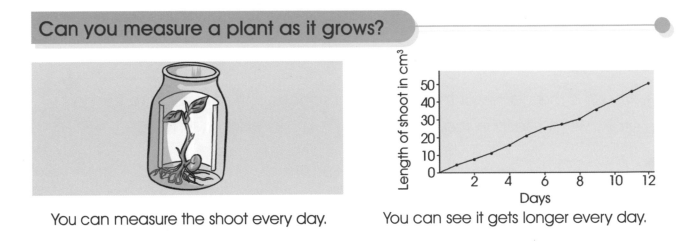

You can measure the shoot every day.

You can see it gets longer every day.

Why should you measure lots of plants?

Every **seedling** grows a little differently. Some grow very well. Others hardly grow at all. They all grow to different heights. What is the best way to record the height?

Seedling number	Shoot length
1	19 mm
2	18 mm
3	21 mm
4	19 mm
5	13 mm
Average	**18 mm**

The best thing is to measure lots of seedlings and take an average. You will be sure your answer is right.

These cress seedlings are all different heights.

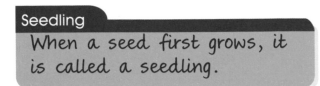

Seed
The small part of a fruit that grows into a new plant.

Seedling
When a seed first grows, it is called a seedling.

Test your learning

On track

1 Efik and Yin are growing some seeds in saucers. They measured the shoots every day. Here is a graph showing the results for one shoot.

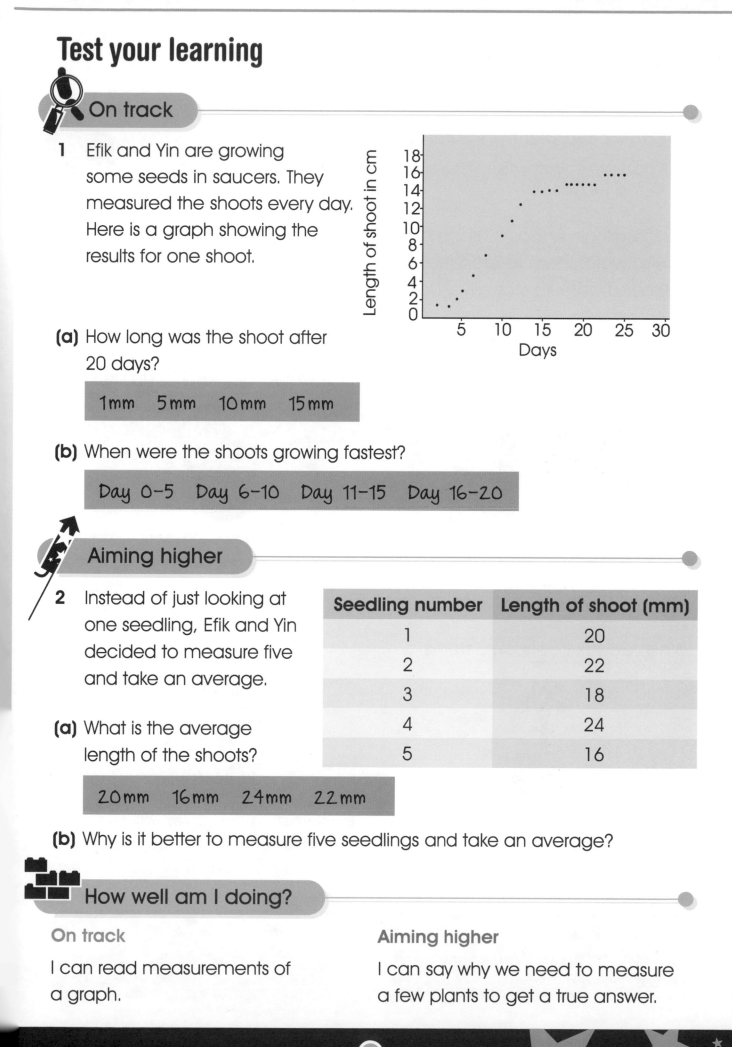

(a) How long was the shoot after 20 days?

| 1 mm | 5 mm | 10 mm | 15 mm |

(b) When were the shoots growing fastest?

| Day 0–5 | Day 6–10 | Day 11–15 | Day 16–20 |

Aiming higher

2 Instead of just looking at one seedling, Efik and Yin decided to measure five and take an average.

Seedling number	Length of shoot (mm)
1	20
2	22
3	18
4	24
5	16

(a) What is the average length of the shoots?

| 20 mm | 16 mm | 24 mm | 22 mm |

(b) Why is it better to measure five seedlings and take an average?

How well am I doing?

On track

I can read measurements of a graph.

Aiming higher

I can say why we need to measure a few plants to get a true answer.

8 Why do plants need water?

- Plants need plenty of water to grow properly.
- Roots take water from the soil, and the stem carries it up to the leaves.

If it doesn't rain enough, all the plants in the garden dry up and die. You have to water them to keep them alive. Flowers in a vase are the same. They need water to stay alive. Nothing can live without water.

How do we know a plant needs water?

Plants cannot grow properly without plenty of water. They just dry up and die.

These beans will never start to grow as long as they stay dry. They need a good soaking to get started.

Look at the way the leaves have gone weak and floppy because there is no water left in the pot. The plant has wilted.

What do the roots and stems do?

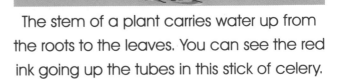

The roots soak up water from the soil. This plant needs a bigger pot so its roots can spread out more. Then it will grow better.

The stem of a plant carries water up from the roots to the leaves. You can see the red ink going up the tubes in this stick of celery.

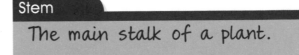

Wilted

A plant has wilted when it droops because it does not have enough water.

Stem

The main stalk of a plant.

Test your learning

On track

1   Jack was growing some seeds in dishes. He kept them under different conditions.

	Water	Light	Did they grow?
Dish 1	yes	yes	yes
Dish 2	yes	no	yes
Dish 3	no	no	no

(a) What does this experiment show that seeds need to grow?

(b) Cecilia's mum's flowers have wilted. They look as if they might die. What is the best thing she could try to get them healthy again?
   • Water them.
   • Put them in a warm place.
   • Put them in a bright place.

Aiming higher

2   Jack's Christmas tree had no roots because it had been chopped down. Cecilia's still had its roots on, and she kept it in a pot of earth. After Christmas they both planted their trees in the garden to use again.

(a) Which tree was the most likely to live?

(b) Why was this tree more likely to survive?
   • It would not fall over.
   • It could take up water better.
   • It still had all its needles.

How well am I doing?

On track

I can say that plants must have water to survive.

Aiming higher

I can explain what a plant's roots and stems are for.

9 Why do plants need warmth?

- Plants will not grow at all if it is too cold.
- You can grow tomatoes better in a warm greenhouse.

Plants need warmth to grow well. Nothing in the garden grows much in the winter. The grass does not need mowing. Seeds do not start to grow until the weather gets warmer in the spring. Everything is waiting for the warm days.

Why do plants need to be warm?

Yin put one lot of seeds in a warm box, and another lot in the cold fridge. They were both in the dark, to make it fair.

The seedlings in the warm place grew much better.

How do gardeners keep things warm?

If we keep our plants warm they grow much faster.

It is much warmer in the **greenhouse**. All the plants in it grow big very quickly.

These lovely tomatoes grew very quickly in the greenhouse.

Fair test
Comparing two things in a way that gives each one an equal chance.

Greenhouse
A building with glass walls and roof. The sun makes it warm inside.

Test your learning

On track

1   The grass in Mr Rossi's garden grows very well in the summer. He has to mow it every week or it gets too long. In the winter it doesn't grow.

(a) What is a reason that the grass grows better in the summer?
- It rains more in the summer.
- Mowing the grass makes it grow faster.
- It is warmer in the summer.

(b) Mr Rossi cannot easily grow grapes in his garden in England, but his sister in Italy grows them very well. Explain why that is.

Aiming higher

2   Mr Rossi grows his tomatoes in a greenhouse. Mrs Novak grows hers outside. Mr Rossi's tomatoes grow much bigger and turn red sooner.

(a) What is the most likely reason that Mr Rossi's plants grow better?

- Mrs Novak's cat is spoiling her plants.
- Plants grow better in the greenhouse.
- It is too windy in Mrs Novak's garden.

(b) Why does a greenhouse help plants to grow well?

How well am I doing?

On track	Aiming higher
I know plants need warmth to grow well.	I can explain that greenhouses help plants grow by keeping them warm.

10 Why do plants need light?

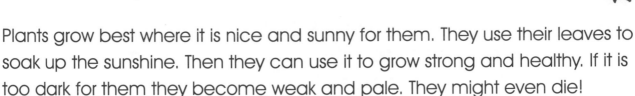

- Plants need sunlight to grow healthily.
- Without leaves a plant cannot grow. It is the leaves that catch the light.

Plants grow best where it is nice and sunny for them. They use their leaves to soak up the sunshine. Then they can use it to grow strong and healthy. If it is too dark for them they become weak and pale. They might even die!

Why do plants need light to grow properly?

Plants growing in the dark grow badly. They are tall and thin. They look yellow and spindly.

The tall yellowish plant has been kept in the dark. It should look like the one that has been growing properly in the light.

Jim has packed up his tent after a week. You can see the grass is pale where it used to be. The grass could not grow in the dark under the tent.

What are the leaves for?

This healthy geranium has all of its leaves. It is growing well.

This geranium has had most of its leaves pulled off. It cannot grow properly.

The plant needs its leaves. They catch the sunlight so the plant can use it to grow healthily. They make food for the plant.

Spindly	Pale
Tall and thin.	A weak colour.

Test your learning

On track

1   Yin noticed that the seedlings do
    not grow very well underneath
    the tree. They do much better
    further away.

(a) Give two different reasons why
    the seedlings grow better further
    away from the tree.

(b) From this list, pick two words that
    would describe the seedlings that
    are trying to grow under the tree.

    yellow   thick   thin   short

Aiming higher

2   The caterpillar is eating the plant
    leaf. Soon the plant will only
    have about half of its leaves left.

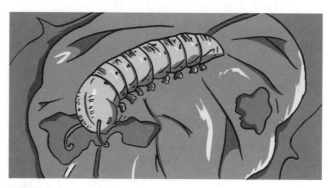

(a) What does losing its leaves do
    to the plant's ability to grow?

(b) What is the job that the leaves normally do for the plant?

How well am I doing?

On track

I know that plants need light to grow
properly.

Aiming higher

I know that the plant's leaves take up
the light it needs to grow.

11 What do we make things with?

- We use many different materials to make things.
- **Some materials are used for many different jobs.**

Do you know what the windows in your house are made of? How about the tables and chairs inside the house? What was used to make the carpets? Complicated objects like cars are made from many different materials.

What materials do you know?

Spectacles and windows are made of glass. So are drinking glasses.

Wood makes good tables and chairs. Doors and floors in houses are often wooden too.

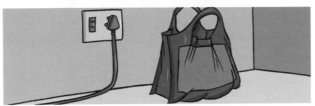

Plastic can be made into bags and buckets. Electric plugs and sockets are also plastic.

There are many different metals to use. Gold is used for rings and iron is for bridges.

What materials are used to make a car?

A car is made from many different **materials**.

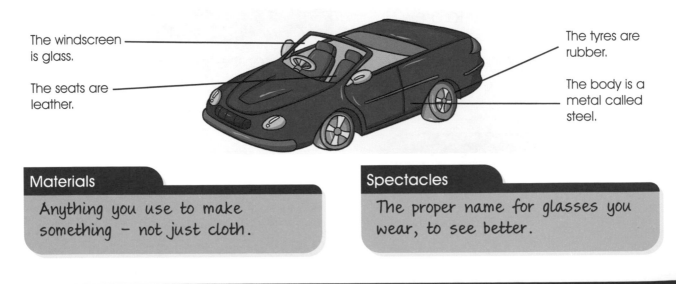

The windscreen is glass.

The seats are leather.

The tyres are rubber.

The body is a metal called steel.

Materials

Anything you use to make something – not just cloth.

Spectacles

The proper name for glasses you wear, to see better.

Test your learning

On track

1   Efik is working at his desk in school.
    He has some things around him.
    They are labelled from A to E.

    These things are made from very
    different materials.

| wood | plastic | wool | cotton | paper |

(a) Match up the labels with the materials. The first one has been done for you.

Letter	Material
A	wood
B	
C	
D	
E	

Aiming higher

2   Some materials can be used for many different jobs. For example, glass can be
    used to make windows, drinking glasses and spectacles.

(a) For each of these materials, try to think of two different uses.

Plastic		Iron	
Job 1	Job 2	Job 1	Job 2
Cotton		Rubber	
Job 1	Job 2	Job 1	Job 2

How well am I doing?

On track

I can name at least six materials used to
make things.

Aiming higher

I can think of at least six different things
made from materials.

12 What materials shall we use?

- Know what an object is for, before deciding what material to make it with.

- There are many different materials that can do the job you need done.

Buckets are often made of plastic. Have you ever wondered why? A plastic bucket holds water without **leaking**. It doesn't go rusty if it gets wet. It doesn't weigh much, so it's easy to carry. It's the perfect thing to hold water!

What is a good material?

A good choice for a teapot

Pottery is a good choice for a teapot. The heat will not melt it, and the water stays in.

A bad choice for a teapot

A chocolate teapot is no good. A teapot has to be able to hold hot tea without **melting**.

Can you use different materials for the same job?

Hats can be made of many different things.

Wool is a good choice for a winter hat. It will keep you nice and warm.

A woolly hat would be too hot in the summer. You need a nice cool hat made of straw to keep the sun off your head.

Leaking

Letting water escape, like a bottle with a hole in it.

Melting

Changing from a solid to a liquid by warming up. Snow melts in the sunshine.

Test your learning

On track

1   Here are some reasons for choosing or not choosing some materials.

> You can't see through it. It is strong. It is too weak.
> It holds water. You can see through it. It would leak.

(a) Match up the reasons to the choices. The first one is done for you.

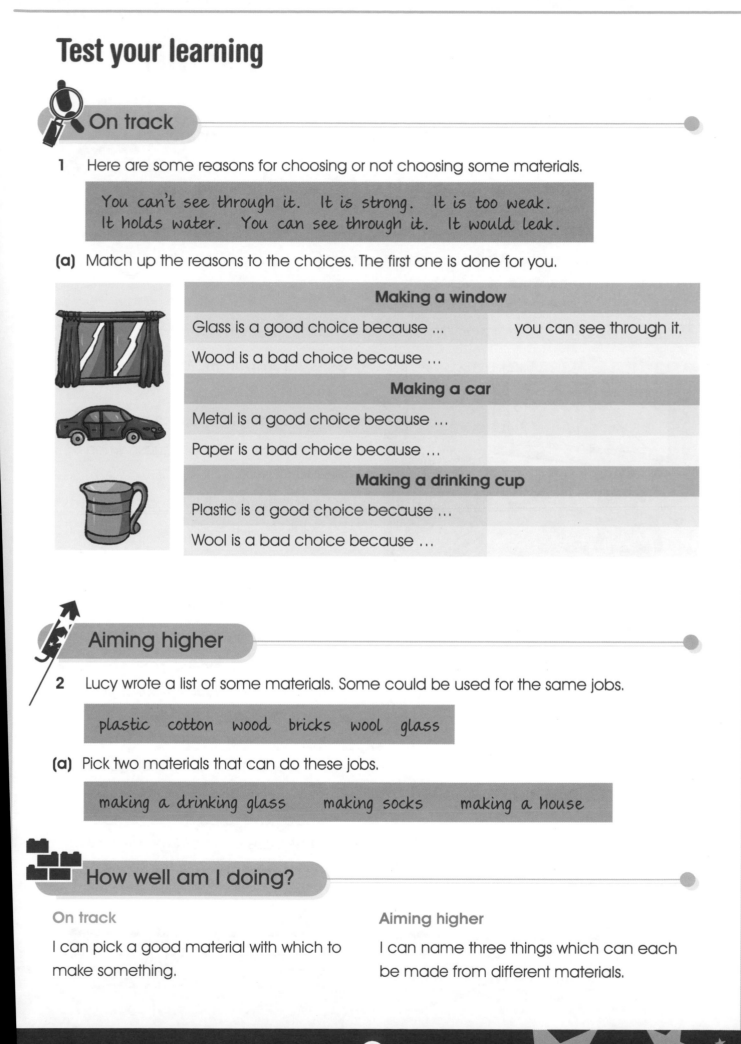

Making a window	
Glass is a good choice because ...	you can see through it.
Wood is a bad choice because ...	
Making a car	
Metal is a good choice because ...	
Paper is a bad choice because ...	
Making a drinking cup	
Plastic is a good choice because ...	
Wool is a bad choice because ...	

Aiming higher

2   Lucy wrote a list of some materials. Some could be used for the same jobs.

> plastic   cotton   wood   bricks   wool   glass

(a) Pick two materials that can do these jobs.

> making a drinking glass   making socks   making a house

How well am I doing?

On track

I can pick a good material with which to make something.

Aiming higher

I can name three things which can each be made from different materials.

13 What makes a material useful?

- Materials have different properties that make them useful for different jobs.
- We use the properties to decide which material to use for a job.

Materials have many different **properties**. The property of a material tells us whether it is stretchy or not, or whether it is waterproof, or something else. If you know the properties of a material, you know what to use it for.

What properties are important?

- Glass is **transparent**. You can see through it.
- Wood is **strong**. It does not break easily.
- Stone is **hard**. It will not squash when you stand on it.
- Rubber is **flexible**. It is bendy, and goes back into shape easily.

How do we make up our mind which material to use?

You can look at a few properties of each material to help you decide.

Properties			
Material	**Transparent**	**Hard**	**Flexible**
wood	no	yes	yes
glass	yes	yes	no
metal	no	yes	yes
wool	no	no	yes
cotton	no	no	yes
ceramic	no	yes	no

What if you wanted to pick a material to make a shirt? Only wool or cotton have the right properties:
- A shirt has to be soft, not hard.
- A shirt has to be flexible (bendy).

If you wanted to make a window, it would have to be made of glass. Glass is the only hard material you can see through. It is transparent.

Waterproof
A waterproof material is one that does not let water through.

Ceramic
Baked clay. Tiles and flower pots are ceramic.

Test your learning

On track

1   Efik and Yin have written out some words to do with materials. Some of the words are the names of materials, and some are properties.

concrete   transparent   strong   ceramic   hard   wool   plastic   flexible

(a)   Sort the words into two lists.

Names of materials	Properties of materials

Aiming higher

2   Efik and Yin thought about the properties needed for different materials.

(a)   Use the letters to match up the properties to the jobs.

A   waterproof   B   transparent   C   flexible
D   strong   E   soft   F   hard

Job	Property of materials
Iron is used to build bridges because it is …	
Glass is used for windows because it is …	
Cotton is used for a T-shirt because it is …	
Rubber is used for wellington boots because it is …	
Stone is used for pavements because it is …	
Leather is used for shoes because it is …	

How well am I doing?

On track

I can name the properties that make a material useful.

Aiming higher

I can decide which material would be good for a particular job.

14 How absorbent are materials?

- To make a good paper towel you need paper that is very **absorbent**.

- If you are comparing different sorts of paper your test must be **fair**.

When you are drying your hands on a paper towel, you want one that will soak up a lot of water. Would any sort of paper be all right to make a towel, or are some better than others? You can test that idea for yourself.

How can you test how good different sorts of paper are at soaking up water?

Panther class counted how many drops of water different types of paper can hold before it starts to drip. They put their results in a table.

Type of paper	How many drops did it hold?
kitchen roll	20
school paper towel	15
tissue	10
newspaper	5

Can you see that kitchen roll was the best?

How can you make sure your test is fair?

I don't think the tissue paper had a fair chance. It was thinner than the kitchen roll.

Jack is quite right. If the paper is too thin it will not be able to hold much water.

To do this test fairly, each piece of paper has to be the same thickness. Then we can really see which is the best.

Absorb

To soak up water.

Absorbency

How well something can soak up water.

RISING ★ STARS

Science Study Guide: Year 3

Answer Booklet

Unit		On track		Aiming higher
1 What types of food are there?	**(a)**	<table><tr><td>fruits and vegetables</td><td>tomato</td></tr><tr><td>meat and fish</td><td>lamb chop</td></tr><tr><td>fats and oils</td><td>olive oil</td></tr><tr><td>sugars and starches</td><td>cake</td></tr></table>	**(a)** **(b)**	Eggs, cheese and meat. Sugars and starches such as bread, rice, pasta and potatoes.
	(b)	Starches and fats		
2 How can eating keep you healthy?	**(a)** **(b)**	He could eat less. He could take more exercise. He could walk faster.	**(a)** **(b)**	Eat lots of different foods. Vegetables
3 What do animals eat?	**(a)** **(b)**	Bar charts with all bars at correct heights. Five	**(a)** **(b)**	Canine teeth cut and tear meat. They act like scissors to cut grass.
4 What teeth have you got?	**(a)**	<table><tr><th>Letter</th><th>Name of tooth</th></tr><tr><td>B</td><td>incisor</td></tr><tr><td>C</td><td>canine</td></tr><tr><td>A</td><td>molar</td></tr></table>	**(a)**	<table><tr><th>Name of tooth</th><th>Job</th></tr><tr><td>incisor</td><td>A</td></tr><tr><td>canine</td><td>C</td></tr><tr><td>molar</td><td>B</td></tr></table>
			(b)	They are sharp.
5 How can you look after your teeth?	**(a)** **(b)** **(c)**	Milk teeth Two Your mouth will get bigger.	**(a)** **(b)**	Avoid sugary drinks which feed the germs that rot teeth. Eat apples and carrots because they don't feed the germs. Brushing teeth cleans off the germs that rot teeth.
6 What plants do we eat?	**(a)** **(b)**	Suitable list of fruits and vegetables Bread, biscuits, pasta.	**(a)**	<table><tr><th>Animal</th><th>What plant does it eat?</th></tr><tr><td>chickens</td><td>mixed grains</td></tr><tr><td>rabbits</td><td>carrots</td></tr><tr><td>ducks</td><td>pondweed</td></tr><tr><td>sheep</td><td>grass</td></tr></table>
			(b)	For his cows to eat – milk comes from cows.
7 How fast do plants grow?	**(a)** **(b)**	15 mm Day 6–10	**(a)** **(b)**	20 mm To get a typical value./To make the results more reliable.
8 Why do plants need water?	**(a)** **(b)**	Water Water them.	**(a)** **(b)**	Lucy's It could take up water better.
9 Why do plants need warmth?	**(a)** **(b)**	It is warmer in the summer. Grapes don't usually grow well in England as it is too cold. They grow well in Italy where it is warm.	**(a)** **(b)**	Plants grow better in the greenhouse. A greenhouse keeps plants warm all the time.

Unit		On track		Aiming higher
10 Why do plants need light?	(a) (b)	They have more light/water. Yellow and thin.	(a) (b)	Without the leaves they cannot catch light from the Sun. They use sunlight to help make food.
11 What do we make things with?	(a)	*See table below*	(a)	**Plastic** – bags/buckets/mugs/toys **Iron** – cars/bridges/ships **Cotton** – shirts/tablecloths/dresses **Rubber** – tyres/erasers/wellington boots
12 What materials shall we use?	(a)	**Window:** Wood is a bad choice because you can't see through it. **Car:** Metal is a good choice because it is strong. Paper is a bad choice because it is too weak. **Drinking cup:** Plastic is a good choice because it holds water. Wool is a bad choice because it would leak.	(a)	Making a drinking glass – glass/ plastic Making socks – cotton/wool Making a house – bricks/wood
13 What makes a material useful?	(a)	**Names of materials:** concrete, ceramic, wool, plastic. **Properties of materials:** transparent, strong, hard, flexible.	(a)	*See table below*
14 How absorbent are materials?	(a) (b)	Absorbency Towel B – the only towel that soaked up all the water.	(a) (b)	To make his test fair. The pieces of towel should be the same thickness.
15 How stretchy are materials?	(a)	Most stretchy : D – B – C – A : least stretchy	(a) (b)	The same size (length) To make it fair
16 What are rocks?	(a)	*See table below*	(a) (b) (c)	Slate – it is waterproof. Sandstone – it is easy to cut and shape. Marble – it is hard wearing and attractive.
	(b)	In nature – on or beneath the Earth's surface.		
	(c)	They are all the same materials. Stones are smaller in size than rocks, pebbles are smaller than stones.		
17 How are rocks different?	(a) (b) (c)	Her fingernail or a matchstick. Beaker of water and a dropper. Vinegar	(a) (b) (c)	Permeable Granite doesn't soak up water, is solid and not in layers, is not reactive with vinegar and feels rough. Slate has layers, marble does not. Marble fizzes with vinegar, slate does not.

Unit 11 (a):

Letter	Material
A	wood
B	wool
C	paper
D	cotton
E	plastic

Unit 13 Aiming higher (a):

Job	Property
iron	D
glass	B
cotton	E
rubber	A
stone	F
feather	C

Unit 16 (a):

Rocks	Not rocks
limestone slate marble	gold concrete brick wood

Unit		On track		Aiming higher
18 Where are rocks found?	**(a)**	granite; sandstone; marble; limestone	**(a)**	The harbour wall; the cliffs; the house walls; the quarry; on the surface of the land
	(b)	They were brought from a quarry.	**(b)**	The sea; the soil; the buildings
	(c)	Erosion is the wearing away of rock by the weather.		
19 What on Earth is soil?	**(a)**	1 Water freezes, expands and starts splitting the rock. 2 Plant roots slowly help to break the rock down further. 3 Over the centuries rocks turn into pebbles, stones and particles of soil. 4 Dead plants add organic matter to the soil making it richer.	**(a)**	The main rock they are formed from might be different; they might have different amounts of different rocks, pebbles and stones; they might have different amounts of organic matter (dead plants).
			(b)	Two suitable pie charts.
			(c)	Grandad's – it has more organic matter and a better mix of the other materials.
20 How do you plan a fair test?	**(a)**	Think of a question to test; write a good prediction; identify the factors to make the test fair; get the equipment.	**(a)**	Four bottles of the same size; balance to weigh out 200 g of soil; 100 cm^3 water; four different soils; stopwatch; pieces of cloth.
	(b)	Which soil is best at soaking up water?	**(b)**	Jack uses 200 g of soil each time; Yin doesn't; Jack uses 100 cm^3 water each time; Yin doesn't.
21 How do you make a conclusion?	**(a)**	Carry out your test; organise your results; think about what your results mean; see if your results match your prediction.	**(a)**	Soil A: $\frac{1}{3}$ sand and $\frac{2}{3}$ clay Soil B: $\frac{1}{3}$ clay and $\frac{2}{3}$ sand Soil C: just sand Soil D: just clay
	(b)		Soil	Time taken to run through		**(b)**	150 cm^3
			sandy	20 s		
			clay	100 s		
			garden	50 s		
22 Why are magnets special?	**(a)**	Bar; horseshoe; disc	**(a)**	From the bottom: N : S : N : S
	(a)	The magnets repel each other.	**(b)**	It would hover above disc 3.
	(b)	The magnets attract each other.		
23 Can you prove something is magnetic?	**(a)**	Iron nail; steel paperclip	**(a)**	Only some metals are magnetic.
	(b)	Any three from: gold; aluminium; brass; copper		
24 How can you test some predictions?	**(a)**	Do magnets attract through all metals? Do magnets lose their magnetism?	**(a)**	Efik predicted, "I expect the longer magnets will be stronger than the shorter ones." Yin predicted, "Magnets will make the paperclip move, no matter what material covers it."
	(b)	Are all magnets equally strong? Are big magnets always stronger than small magnets? Do magnets work through different materials?	**(b)**	Efik's results show that some shorter magnets are stronger than longer magnets. Yin's results shows that magnetism works through all materials that are not magnetic.
			(c)	Yin's prediction was not true. Efik's prediction was incorrect.

Unit		On track		Aiming higher
25 How stretchy are elastic bands?	(a) (b)	If I stretch an elastic band downwards, I will feel a pull **upwards** on my hand. **Large** pulls make an elastic band stretch **further** than small ones.	(a) (b)	Yes. The results show that as the elastic band is pulled back the distance the toy car travels increases. The bigger the pull on the elastic band the longer the toy car travels.
26 How are shadows formed?	(a) (b)	No. 3: the teddy with the face on it. No. 1: the shadow of the teddy which is dark and the same shape as the teddy.	(a) (b)	1 Light from my projector travels towards Teddy and the screen. 2 Teddy blocks some light. 3 Some light hits Teddy's front and doesn't go any further. 4 Some light travels both sides of Teddy and makes the screen bright. 5 Behind Teddy a shadow is formed where no light shines. A projector or a torch
27 How do shadows change?	(a) (b)	B : C : D : A The Sun is highest at midday. The lower the Sun the longer the shadow.	(a) (b) (c)	140 cm 180 cm 9 a.m. and 3 p.m.
28 Does the Sun really move?	(a) (b)	Around midday. At the right places in the arc that the Sun appears to make.	(a) (b) (c)	Appearing to move (even though he is standing still) The Earth spins on its axis. As the Earth spins the Sun appears to move across the sky. Suitable diagram with Jack in the same position as Efik, having turned about 45 degrees to his left.
29 Which materials make the best shadows?	(a) (b) (c)	Opaque: wood, tinfoil Translucent: bubble wrap, greaseproof paper Transparent: glass, clingfilm Wood and tinfoil block the most light. Opaque: drawing of a dark shadow. Translucent: drawing of a faint shadow. Transparent: drawing of a very faint shadow. Check all are appropriate shapes.	(a) (b) (c)	Different materials let different amounts of light through. Thin cloth, tracing paper, coloured plastic. Even transparent materials block some light.

Test your learning

On track

1 Jack wanted to know which sort of towel is the best to use after a bath.

He decided to pour some water onto four different towels and watch it drip off afterwards.

Towel	Observation
A	Most of the water dripped off.
B	All of the water soaked in.
C	Just a little water dripped off.
D	About half of the water dripped off.

(a) Which property was he testing?

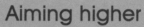
softness   absorbency   flexibility

(b) Which towel would be the best one? Explain why you have chosen it.

Aiming higher

2 When he was doing his towel test, Jack made sure that he used exactly the same amount of water each time. Each piece of towel had exactly one small cup of water poured onto it.

(a) Explain why Jack had to give each towel the same amount of water.

(b) Are there any other things that Jack should have kept the same every time?

How well am I doing?

On track

I can describe how to do a test for absorbency.

Aiming higher

I can say what you need to keep the same each time.

15 How stretchy are materials?

- The material you make socks with has to be **stretchy** so they fit well.

- If you are comparing different sorts of material your test must be fair.

Have you noticed that some socks stay up nicely and others are always falling down? If they are made of stretchy material they grip better. Collect a few different socks. Then you can test which ones are made of the stretchiest material.

How can you compare how stretchy different socks are?

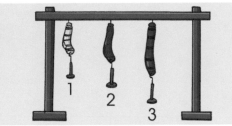

Lucy hung up three different socks with the same weight hanging from each.

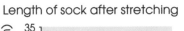
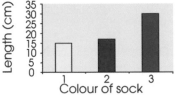

The **bar chart** shows how three different socks have stretched differently, even though they all have the same mass on them.

How can we make sure the test is fair?

Lucy doesn't think the test was fair!

The yellow sock was hers and the blue sock was her dad's. Her dad's sock was much bigger to start with.

All of the socks have to be the same size at the beginning of the test. That is the only way to make it fair.

Stretchy

Something is stretchy if it gets longer when you pull on it.

Bar chart

A way of showing measurements in picture form.

Test your learning

On track

1 Efik and Lucy tested four different fabrics to see which are the most stretchy. They hung 100g masses on each sample of fabric and measured to what length each one stretched. They put their results in a bar chart.

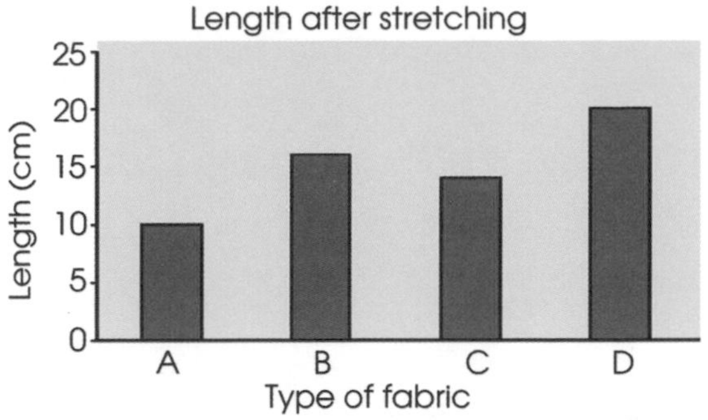

Length after stretching

(Bar chart: y-axis "Length (cm)" from 0 to 25; x-axis "Type of fabric" with bars A = 10, B = 16, C = 14, D = 20)

(a) Look at the bar chart above and put the four types of fabric in order of stretchiness, starting with the most stretchy.

Most stretchy ☐ ☐ ☐ ☐ Least stretchy

Aiming higher

2 Efik and Lucy are talking about their test.

The different fabrics are not the same colour. Does that matter?

I don't think so. But we should make sure everything else is the same!

(a) Name one thing that they should keep the same for each piece of fabric.

(b) Why is it important to keep this thing (factor) the same every time?

How well am I doing?

On track

I can describe a stretchiness test.

Aiming higher

I can explain how to make the test fair.

16 What are rocks?

- There are many different kinds of **rocks**.
- **Different properties make rocks useful for different jobs.**

Rocks are a kind of material found in nature. Stones and pebbles are just smaller pieces of a rock. Rocks are often used in buildings. Other materials such as bricks and concrete are not rocks because they are man-made.

What rocks might you see where you live?

Jack saw different kinds of rocks used in buildings near his school.

Marble is often used as tiles or slabs.

Sandstone is used to build church walls.

Slate is used as a roofing material.

Limestone is also used to build walls.

What properties make these rocks useful?

Jack's table shows the useful properties of four rocks.

Rock	Useful properties
marble	hardwearing and attractive to look at
sandstone	has an even texture and is easy to cut and shape
slate	waterproof and easy to split into sheets
limestone	attractive but wears away more quickly

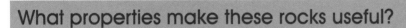

Waterproof

A rock that is resistant to water.

Rock

Hard materials that make up the Earth's crust.

Test your learning

On track

1 Jack collected different materials. Some were rocks – some weren't.

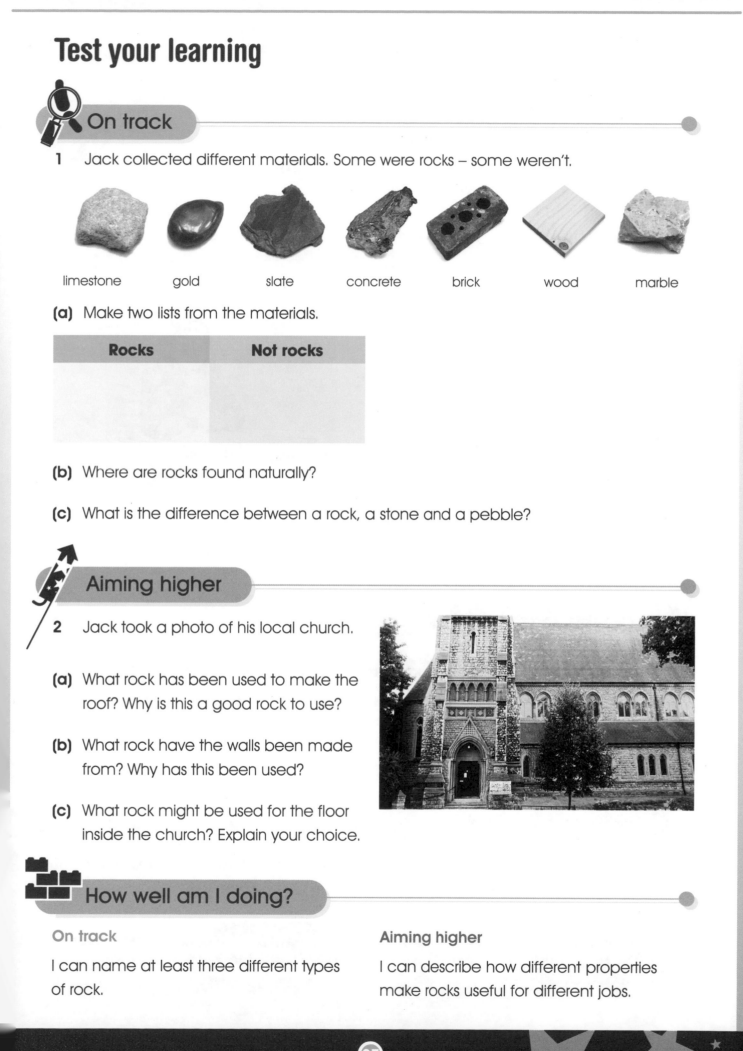

limestone   gold   slate   concrete   brick   wood   marble

(a) Make two lists from the materials.

Rocks	Not rocks

(b) Where are rocks found naturally?

(c) What is the difference between a rock, a stone and a pebble?

Aiming higher

2 Jack took a photo of his local church.

(a) What rock has been used to make the roof? Why is this a good rock to use?

(b) What rock have the walls been made from? Why has this been used?

(c) What rock might be used for the floor inside the church? Explain your choice.

How well am I doing?

On track

I can name at least three different types of rock.

Aiming higher

I can describe how different properties make rocks useful for different jobs.

17 How are rocks different?

- You can test rocks to see how different they are.
- Tables of information help you compare properties.

Some rocks are hard, others are soft. They might feel rough or smooth. Some soak up water, others split into sheets when you hit them. A few fizz when you add some vinegar.

What test can you do on rocks?

Yin did some tests on four different rocks.

Test 1 Hardness
"I scratched each rock with my fingernail, a coin, a matchstick and a plastic knife."

Test 2 Permeability
"I dropped some water onto each rock to see if the water soaked in."

Test 3 Structure
"I looked at each rock to see if it was made of flat layers."

Test 4 Reactivity
"I put a few drops of vinegar on each rock to see if it fizzed or not."

What did the scratch test show?

Rock	What made a mark when used to scratch the rock?			
	fingernail	coin	matchstick	plastic knife
marble	✗	✓	✗	✗
sandstone	✗	✓	✗	✓
granite	✗	✗	✗	✗
slate	✗	✓	✗	✗

Granite was the hardest rock – nothing scratched it! Sandstone was the softest. The coin and the plastic knife both scratched it.

Permeable
The ability to let water soak through.

Observation
What you see happening in a test.

Test your learning

On track

1   Here is some equipment Yin used in her tests.

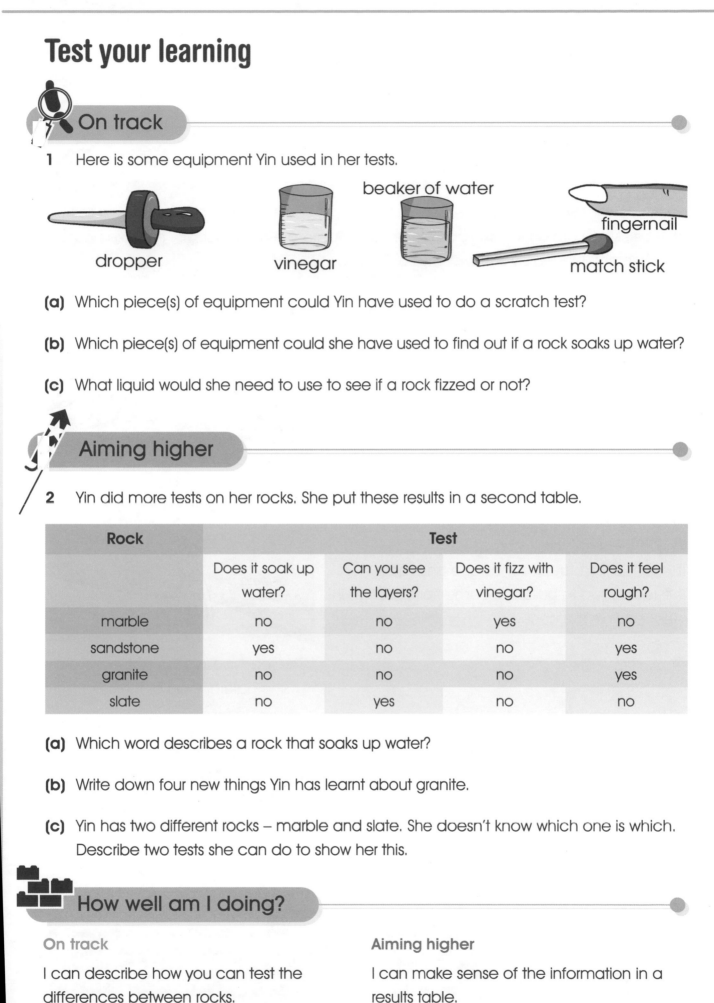

dropper   vinegar   beaker of water   fingernail   match stick

(a) Which piece(s) of equipment could Yin have used to do a scratch test?

(b) Which piece(s) of equipment could she have used to find out if a rock soaks up water?

(c) What liquid would she need to use to see if a rock fizzed or not?

Aiming higher

2   Yin did more tests on her rocks. She put these results in a second table.

Rock	Test			
	Does it soak up water?	Can you see the layers?	Does it fizz with vinegar?	Does it feel rough?
marble	no	no	yes	no
sandstone	yes	no	no	yes
granite	no	no	no	yes
slate	no	yes	no	no

(a) Which word describes a rock that soaks up water?

(b) Write down four new things Yin has learnt about granite.

(c) Yin has two different rocks – marble and slate. She doesn't know which one is which. Describe two tests she can do to show her this.

How well am I doing?

On track

I can describe how you can test the differences between rocks.

Aiming higher

I can make sense of the information in a results table.

18 Where are rocks found?

- Some rocks are easily seen but others are hidden.
- There are always rocks under the surface of the ground.

Have you ever wondered where people find rocks? Most have been around for millions of years. Many are on the **surface** of the Earth. Some are hard to spot – they are under the Earth and hidden by soil, buildings or the sea.

Where might you see some rocks?

In the countryside

The Highlands of Scotland are covered in granite rock. Wind, rain and ice have helped shape the landscape over many centuries.

In town

This statue is made of sandstone and marble. The rocks used to build this came from quarries in other parts of the country.

At the seaside

Durdle Door is a famous landmark in Dorset. Most of what you see is limestone rock. Over many centuries the sea has **eroded** it into the shape it is today.

What hides rocks?

Grass and soil hide
the underground rocks.

The road around the statue covers
the natural rocks of the area.

The sea covers the rocks
on the seabed.

Erosion
The wearing away of land by wind, water or ice.

Surface
The topmost part of a material.

Rocks and soils   18 Where are rocks found?

Test your learning

On track

1   Think about the rocks in the drawings of the Scottish mountains, the statue and Durdle Door.

(a) Name the four rocks shown in these drawings.

(b) Where did the rocks in the statue come from?

(c) Explain what erosion is.

Aiming higher

2   Jack found a drawing showing lots of rocks.

(a) Name four different places where you can see rocks in Jack's drawing.

(b) Name three things which are covering or hiding rocks.

How well am I doing?

On track

I can explain why you can see rocks in some pictures but not others.

Aiming higher

I can name three things which hide underground rocks from us.

41

19 What on Earth is soil?

- Soil comes from rocks.
- Different rocks produce different soils.

Over millions of years, rocks are worn down into soil. The **rock particles** get smaller, and more and more **dead plant** (organic) **matter** is added. Different soils contain different-sized particles and different amounts of organic matter.

How is soil formed?

1. Frost shatters rock. When water freezes in the cracks in rock, it makes the rock **split** or even **shatter**.

2. Plants add to the breakdown. Plant roots are strong enough to break open some rocks.

3. Flowing water turns the rock to pebbles. The rocks knock together and break, and get smaller and smaller. The smallest bits become **sand**.

4. Organic matter is added. When plants die, they rot, adding **organic matter** to the soil. That helps other plants grow well.

What makes soils different from each other?

There are different kinds of soil because:
- the main rock they are formed from may be different
- different soils are mixtures of different rocks
- some soil might have a lot of organic matter – another might have very little.

Frost

Ice crystals forming a white deposit.

Organic matter

Material formed from dead animals or plants.

Test your learning

On track

1 Jack has made a list which shows how soils are formed. It is in the wrong order.

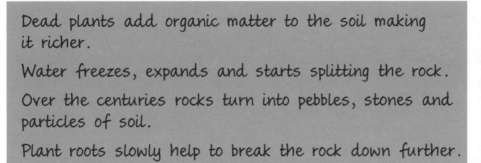

> Dead plants add organic matter to the soil making it richer.
>
> Water freezes, expands and starts splitting the rock.
>
> Over the centuries rocks turn into pebbles, stones and particles of soil.
>
> Plant roots slowly help to break the rock down further.

(a) Rewrite Jack's list in the correct order.

Aiming higher

2 Jack had some soil from his garden and some from his granddad's. He separated the portions of soil into their different parts. The table shows what each contained.

	Jack's soil	Granddad's soil
chalk	10g	20g
clay	50g	10g
sand	30g	40g
gravel	5g	15g
organic material	5g	15g

(a) Write down three reasons why the soils might be different from each other.

(b) Use Jack's data to make two pie charts showing how each portion of soil is made up.

(c) Which soil might be best at growing plants?

How well am I doing?

On track

I can describe how soil is formed.

Aiming higher

I can explain what makes one soil different from another.

20 How do you plan a fair test?

- Questions and predictions come at the start of an investigation.

- Tests have to be as fair as they can.

Can you put a complete **fair test** together yet? Panther class are working on this. They want to test how quickly water can drain through different soils. Their first job is to think about how to plan a test and make sure it is fair.

What did Mrs Novak's Panther class do at the start of their test?

First identify a question you can test in the classroom: "Does water drain equally fast through all soils?"

Then write down your prediction: "Water will drain more quickly through sandy soils than clay soils."

Mrs Novak

How did they make sure their test was fair?

Panther class put different soils into similar bottles. A piece of cloth stops the soil falling out. Water is put in at the top and drips into the bottom of the bottle. They measured how long it takes for the water to drain through.

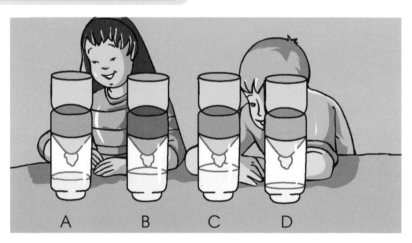

To make their test fair they made sure they had the same amount of soil each time. They used the same amount of water and the same size of cloth each time as well.

Fair test

A test which keeps everything the same except for the thing you are testing.

Factor

Something that might affect the result of a fair test.

Test your learning

On track

1   Jack drew a chart to show the stages in his plan. But it was wrong!

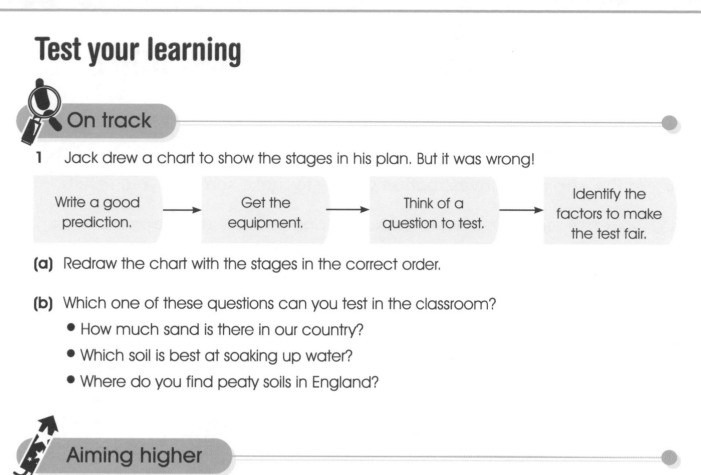

| Write a good prediction. | → | Get the equipment. | → | Think of a question to test. | → | Identify the factors to make the test fair. |

(a)   Redraw the chart with the stages in the correct order.

(b)   Which one of these questions can you test in the classroom?

  • How much sand is there in our country?

  • Which soil is best at soaking up water?

  • Where do you find peaty soils in England?

Aiming higher

2   Yin and Jack wanted to know how quickly water would drain through different soils. They each made a plan for their fair test. One is better than the other.

	Yin's plan	Jack's plan
Step 1	I will put different soils in each of my four bottles.	I will put 200 g of different soils in each of my four bottles.
Step 2	I'll pour a bit of water into each bottle.	I will pour 100 cm³ of water into each bottle.
Step 3	I will compare how long it takes for 50 cm³ of water to go through.	I will compare how long it takes for 50 cm³ of water to go through.

(a)   Write down a list of equipment needed to do this test.

(b)   Look at Yin and Jack's plans. Give two ways in which Jack's plan is fairer than Yin's.

How well am I doing?

On track

I can describe what to do in starting to plan a fair test.

Aiming higher

I can decide if a test is fair or not.

21 How do you make a conclusion?

- Before you can make a **conclusion** you have to organise your **results**.

- At the end of an **investigation** you try to make sense of your results.

Can you make sense of test results? Mrs Novak's class discusses what their results on soil drainage mean. Do their results make any sense?

How did Panther class organise their results?

Panther class did their test. They measured how long it took for 50 cm³ of water to drain through four different soils.

They wondered how best to organise their results. Mrs Novak said, "In this case it makes sense to put them in a **table** rather than a **graph**, **pie chart** or **bar chart**."

Kind of soil	Time taken for 50 cm³ of water to go through soil
all sand	50 seconds
mostly sand, some clay	150 seconds
mostly clay, some sand	200 seconds
all clay	300 seconds

Do the results make any sense?

Mrs Novak asked Yin and Jack to see if there was any **pattern** in the results.

Yin:
"The results show water goes fastest through sand and slowest through clay."

Jack:
"Adding sand to clay **reduces** the time it takes for the water to go through."

Mrs Novak:
"Finally, you can see how well your results match your prediction."

Prediction:
"Water will drain more quickly through sandy soils than clay soils."

Yes. Our results fit the prediction very well. There are bigger spaces between sand particles than between clay particles. So sandy soil drains fastest.

Results

Data measured in a scientific test or investigation.

Conclusion

A scientific fact or idea based on experimental evidence.

Test your learning

On track

1   Yin mixed up the final stages in her test.

| Organise your results. | → | See if your results match your prediction. | → | Think about what your results mean. | → | Carry out your test. |

(a) Redraw the chart with the stages in the right order.

Jack said, "My first type of soil was sandy and the water took 20s to run through. My clay soil took 100s. The soil from my garden was in-between – it took 50s."

(b) Organise these results into a proper table.

Aiming higher

2   Jack and Yin measured how much water flows through different soils in three minutes. They used the same equipment as before. The bar chart shows their results.

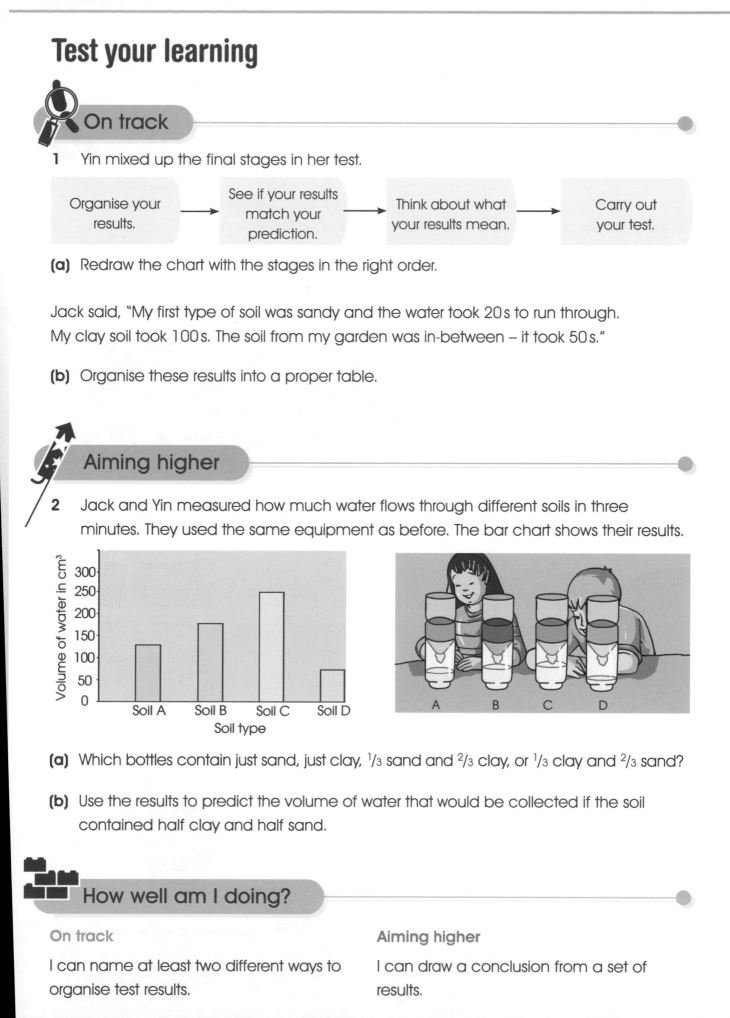

(a) Which bottles contain just sand, just clay, $\frac{1}{3}$ sand and $\frac{2}{3}$ clay, or $\frac{1}{3}$ clay and $\frac{2}{3}$ sand?

(b) Use the results to predict the volume of water that would be collected if the soil contained half clay and half sand.

How well am I doing?

On track

I can name at least two different ways to organise test results.

Aiming higher

I can draw a conclusion from a set of results.

22 Why are magnets special?

- **Magnets** come in different shapes and sizes.
- **Magnets** produce **forces** and can **attract** or **repel** each other.

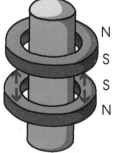

How many different magnets have you seen? Magnets have special properties. An **invisible force** surrounds them which attracts or repels other magnets. If you hold two magnets together you can feel the forces working.

What do magnets look like?

Horseshoe and bar magnets are the most common shapes. They come in other shapes as well. Every magnet has a **North** and a **South pole**.

1 a wand magnet   3 a horseshoe magnet

2 a bar magnet   4 a disc magnet

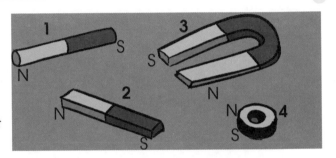

What happens when you hold magnets close to each other?

The poles of a magnet are the ends where the force is strongest. These **bar magnets** can either attract (move towards) or repel each other (push each other apart). This depends on how the poles of each magnet are arranged.

If you bring a North and a South pole together they will attract each other. If the poles are the same, they will repel each other.

These **disc magnets** also have poles, but they are on the flat sides.

When two are placed on this stick with like poles together, they hover above each other. The **like poles** move the magnets apart. They repel each other.

Attract

Exert a force on an object, making it move closer.

Repel

Exert a force on an object, making it move away.

Test your learning

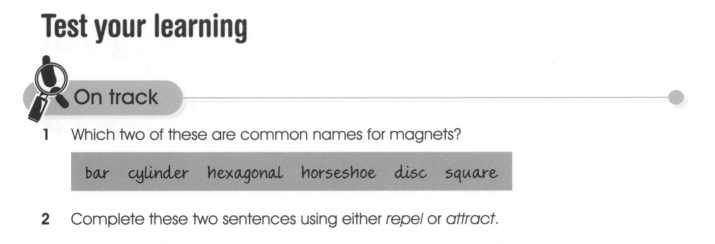

On track

1   Which two of these are common names for magnets?

> bar   cylinder   hexagonal   horseshoe   disc   square

2   Complete these two sentences using either *repel* or *attract*.

(a)   The North pole of a bar magnet is held near the North pole of another bar magnet.
The magnets . . . . each other.

(b)   The South pole of a bar magnet is held near the North pole of another bar magnet.
The magnets . . . . each other.

Aiming higher

3   Jack has drawn three disc magnets.
Disc 3 is floating above the other two.
He has labeled the poles on disc 3.

(a)   Draw the diagram again. Label the
North (N) and South (S) poles on discs
1 and 2.

(b)   What would happen if you put another
disc magnet on top with its South pole
facing upwards?

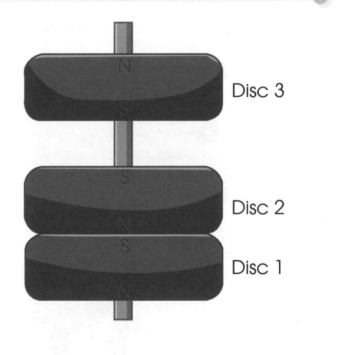

Disc 3

Disc 2

Disc 1

How well am I doing?

On track

I can name four different kinds of magnets.

Aiming higher

Explain what happens when you bring
magnets together.

23 Can you prove something is magnetic?

- Only three different metals can be used to make magnets.
- You can test materials to see if they are **magnetic** or not.

Not many materials can be turned into magnets. Most magnets are made from **iron** (or **steel**) but they can also be made of the metals **cobalt** or **nickel**. No other material is magnetic. Tests prove this.

Which materials are magnetic?

A magnetic material is one that can be attracted to a magnet. Out of all these materials only the steel paperclip is magnetic. None of the others are picked up by a magnet. These are **non-magnetic**. Even the **gold** ring and **copper** bracelet are non-magnetic.

How can you test for a magnet?

Can you remember the rule, "Two magnets attract or repel each other"? Here is a new rule: "A magnet and a magnetic material only attract each other – they never repel."

Magnets only attract magnetic materials.

You can prove a material is magnetic or not by seeing if a magnet picks it up.

Magnetic material	Non-magnetic material
A material which can be attracted to a magnet.	A material which has no magnetic properties.

Test your learning

On track

1   Jack collected various metal objects.

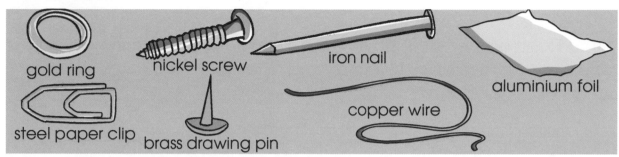

gold ring   nickel screw   iron nail   aluminium foil

steel paper clip   brass drawing pin   copper wire

(a) Which two of these will be attracted by a magnet?

(b) Write down three materials that are non-magnetic.

Aiming higher

2   Jack tested some other materials to see if they were magnetic or not.

Material	Attracted by magnet
plastic ruler	no
brass drawing pin	no
nickel screw	yes
aluminium kitchen foil	no
wooden match	no
copper wire	no
a rubber	no
iron nail	yes

(a) Which of these sentences correctly describes what Jack found out?

All metals are magnetic.
Iron is magnetic but other metals aren't.
Plastic and wood are magnetic.
Only some metals are magnetic.
Brass is a magnetic metal.

How well am I doing?

On track

I can name three magnetic and three non-magnetic materials.

Aiming higher

I can describe how to test if a material is magnetic.

24 How can you test some predictions?

- You can make many **predictions** about magnets.
- Not all predictions turn out to be true.

You can test magnets to find out how strong they are, how far you can feel the magnetic force, and if the force travels through different materials. The **test results** will show if your predictions are good ones.

What questions can you test?

Panther class tested some interesting questions.

Jack

Test 1
Are all magnets equally strong?

Efik

Test 2
Are long magnets always stronger than short magnets?

Test 3
Do magnets work through different materials?

Yin

What predictions did they make?

Their predictions seemed sensible.

Jack predicted, "Magnets can be different strengths. The strongest magnet will hold lots more paperclips than the weakest one."

I will see how many paperclips four different-sized magnets can hold in a chain.

Efik predicted, "I expect the longer magnets will be stronger than the shorter ones."

I will see how close my magnets have to be to a paperclip before it moves.

Yin predicted, "Magnets will make the paperclip move, no matter what material covers it."

I will see if a magnet attracts a paperclip if it is covered by other materials.

Evidence
Observations that help you test a prediction and form a conclusion.

Test
A way of finding things out.

Test your learning

On track

1 Panther class have some other questions about magnets.

> Do magnets attract through all metals?
> What is the biggest magnet in the world?
> When were magnets first discovered?
> Do magnets lose their magnetism?

(a) Which two questions in the above list could they test in the classroom?

(b) What three questions did Panther class test on the opposite page?

Aiming higher

2 Efik and Yin did their tests. Here are their results.

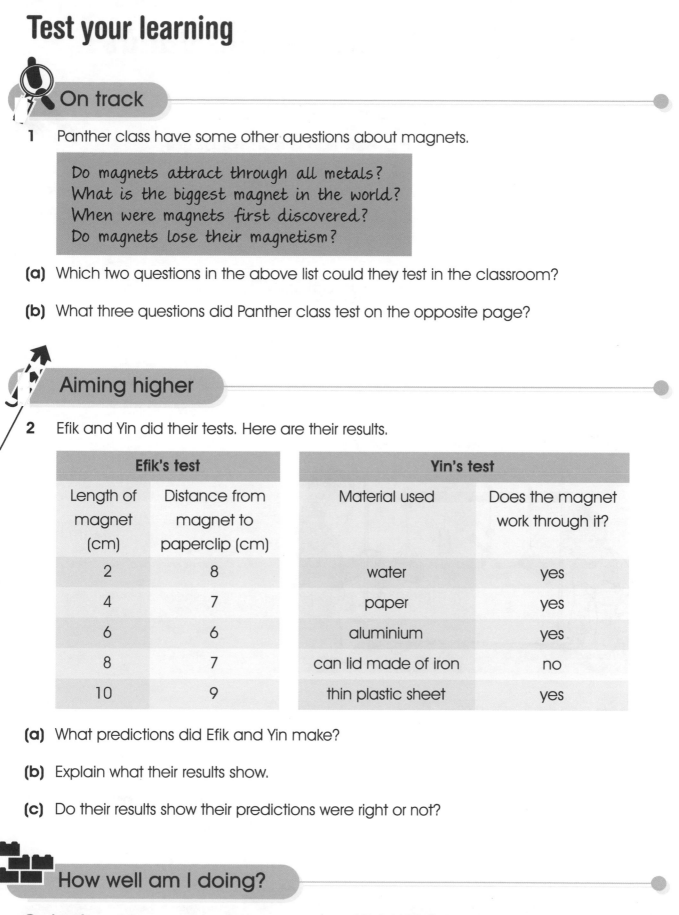

Efik's test		Yin's test	
Length of magnet (cm)	Distance from magnet to paperclip (cm)	Material used	Does the magnet work through it?
2	8	water	yes
4	7	paper	yes
6	6	aluminium	yes
8	7	can lid made of iron	no
10	9	thin plastic sheet	yes

(a) What predictions did Efik and Yin make?

(b) Explain what their results show.

(c) Do their results show their predictions were right or not?

How well am I doing?

On track

I know what tests one can do with magnets.

Aiming higher

I can spot a prediction and use results to see if they fit.

25 How stretchy are elastic bands?

- You can predict how elastic bands might stretch.
- Your results will show if your prediction is correct or not.

Imagine you are stretching some elastic bands. You will feel a **pulling force**. A big force seems to make the band stretch a lot more than a little force. You can test this idea. Test results help you check how good your prediction is.

How did Panther class test their prediction?

Mrs Novak said, "What would happen if different-sized weights were placed on similar elastic bands?"

Most of the class predicted, "The bigger the weight, the longer the band will stretch."

Efik and Lucy show you how they did their test.

This table shows the objects they weighed.

	Weight (N)
scissors	3
shoe	7
book	9
stapler	5

Do the results fit Panther class's prediction?

Efik wrote down:
- Adding a weight makes the elastic band stretch.
- The book is heaviest (9 N) and makes the elastic band stretch the furthest.
- The scissors are lightest and make the elastic band stretch the least.
- Our prediction looks good!

Force

A push, a pull, a twist or a turn.

Rule

A simple statement that describes a scientific pattern.

Test your learning

On track

1   Complete these sentences choosing from these words.

> further   upwards   downwards   large

(a)   If I stretch an elastic band downwards, I will feel a pull . . . . on my hand.

(b)   . . . . pulls make an elastic band stretch . . . . than small ones.

Aiming higher

2   Mrs Novak showed Panther class how to make a toy car move, using an elastic band catapult. Efik predicted, "The car goes further the more the elastic band is pulled back."

Here are Efik's results.

Distance elastic band is pulled back (cm)	Distance the toy car traveled (cm)
2	20
4	60
6	100
8	150

(a)   Do the results show if Efik's prediction is correct? Explain your answer.

(b)   Write out the sentence below choosing the correct words to show a rule he has discovered.
"The bigger/smaller the pull on the elastic band the shorter/longer the toy car travels."

How well am I doing?

On track

I can describe how elastic bands stretch when different weights are added.

Aiming higher

I can use results to see whether a prediction is correct or not.

26 How are shadows formed?

- **Shadows** are similar in shape to the objects forming them.
- **Shadows** are formed when light from a source is blocked.

What do you know about shadows? Shadows are dark and have the same shape as the object that formed them. They are made when light is blocked. You see them on the opposite side of an object from the **light source**.

What do shadows look like?

Jack shone a torch on his hand and a comb and made some shadows.

> The shadow of the comb is dark. It is a similar shape to my comb. I can make it change size if I move it nearer to the wall.

How did Lucy show how light was blocked?

Lucy put her teddy bear between the **projector** and the screen. She turned the projector on.

> My projector is a light source. Light from it travels towards Teddy. Some light travels straight to the screen and lights it up. Some of it hits Teddy. He blocks that light from hitting the screen. It is this part that looks dark and forms the shadow.

Shadow

A dark image formed when an object blocks beams of light.

Light source

An object which gives off its own light beams.

Test your learning

On track

1   Lucy drew three pictures.

(a) Which one is Lucy's view of Teddy?

(b) Which one does she see on the screen?

Aiming higher

2   Lucy described how the teddy bear's shadow was formed. Her sentences are in the
wrong order.

> • Some light hits Teddy's front and doesn't go any further.
> • Some light travels both sides of Teddy and makes the screen bright.
> • Teddy blocks some light.
> • Light from my projector travels towards Teddy and the screen.
> • Behind Teddy a shadow is formed where no light shines.

(a) Rewrite Lucy's sentences in the right order to explain how a shadow is formed.

(b) Name two light sources Lucy could use to make Teddy's shadow.

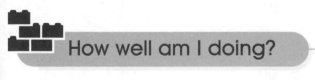

How well am I doing?

On track

I can draw what I think the shadow of an
unfamiliar object might look like.

Aiming higher

I can explain how shadows are formed
using the idea of light beams.

27 How do shadows change?

- Shadows from the Sun change in size and direction during the day.

- Measuring the length of the Sun's shadow helps you tell the time.

Have you heard people say they can tell the time of the day using the Sun? They do it by looking at the shadows the Sun makes. The length and position of the Sun's shadow depends on the time of the day.

How does the Sun's shadow change during the day?

Yin stands in the same spot in the playground at different times of the day. Jack draws her shadow each time and measures its length. In the picture we see them late in the afternoon.

- At dawn the Sun was in the East – the shadow was very long.

- The shortest shadow was seen at midday – the Sun was highest in the sky.

- During the morning the shadow shortens – by the afternoon they are getting longer.

- At sunset the Sun will be in the West – the shadow will be very long again.

Can the Sun's shadow help you predict the time?

Jack recorded the length of Yin's shadow and the time they were made.

Time	7 a.m.	10 a.m.	12 a.m.	?	5 p.m.
Length of shadow (cm)	400	250	150	250	400

There is a pattern in the results!
They get shorter up to midday and then longer again.
I think it will be 2 p.m. when the shadow is 250 cm
long in the afternoon.

Sunrise

The time of the morning when the Sun rises above the horizon.

Sunset

The time of the evening when the Sun drops below the horizon.

Test your learning

On track

1   Jack put a long stick in the playground. He drew the shadows formed at different times of the day. But his drawings got mixed up!

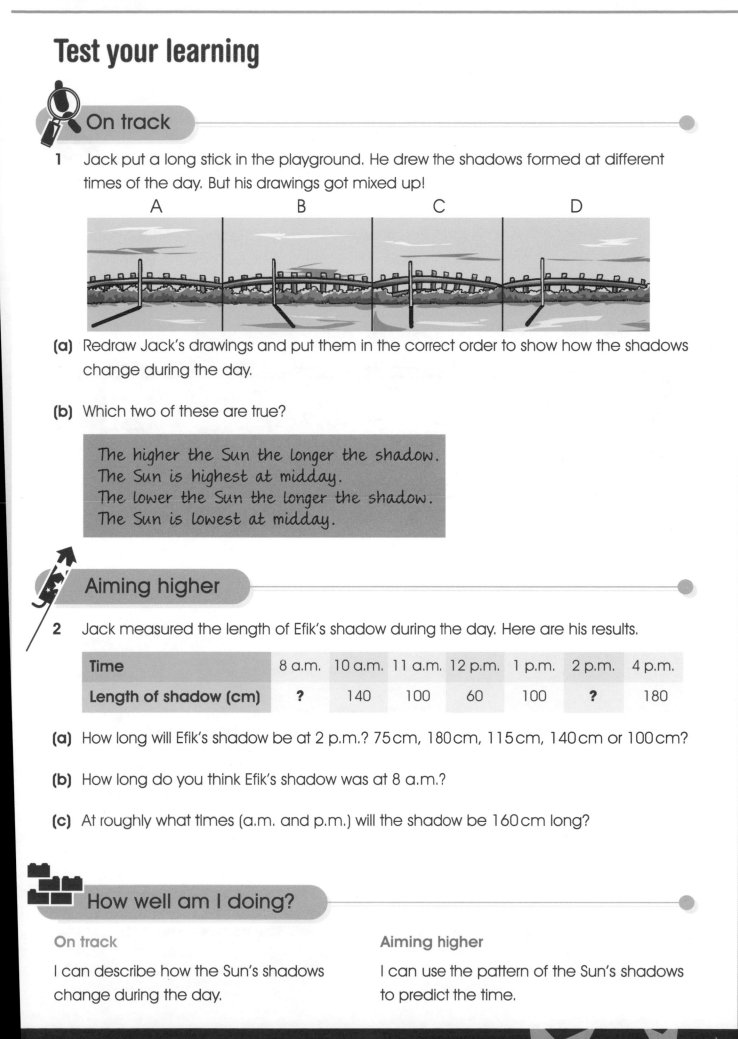

A   B   C   D

(a) Redraw Jack's drawings and put them in the correct order to show how the shadows change during the day.

(b) Which two of these are true?

> The higher the Sun the longer the shadow.
> The Sun is highest at midday.
> The lower the Sun the longer the shadow.
> The Sun is lowest at midday.

Aiming higher

2   Jack measured the length of Efik's shadow during the day. Here are his results.

Time	8 a.m.	10 a.m.	11 a.m.	12 p.m.	1 p.m.	2 p.m.	4 p.m.
Length of shadow (cm)	?	140	100	60	100	?	180

(a) How long will Efik's shadow be at 2 p.m.? 75 cm, 180 cm, 115 cm, 140 cm or 100 cm?

(b) How long do you think Efik's shadow was at 8 a.m.?

(c) At roughly what times (a.m. and p.m.) will the shadow be 160 cm long?

How well am I doing?

On track

I can describe how the Sun's shadows change during the day.

Aiming higher

I can use the pattern of the Sun's shadows to predict the time.

28 Does the Sun really move?

- The **Sun** appears to move during the day in a regular way.

- The Sun looks as if it moves but it is the Earth that moves, not the Sun.

Here is a tricky question – does the Sun actually move across the sky? It certainly looks that way, but is it true? Another way of looking at it is to think about how the Earth moves. This can also explain what we see.

How does the Sun appear to move during the day?

Panther class stuck some stickers on the window. It looks as if the Sun moves across the sky in a regular way. It is highest at midday.

Does the Sun actually move?

At first glance it looks as if the Sun is moving across the sky. In reality it stays still.

Lucy shines a torch on a globe. This represents the Sun shining on Earth. Efik has stuck a figure of a man on the globe. As he turns the globe, the man moves round.

This is what happens in real life. The Sun only looks as if it moves across the sky. If you were the man and looking at the Sun you would think the Sun was moving.

Lucy and Efik help explain how the Earth's movement makes it look as if the Sun moves.

Sun

The star at the centre of our solar system.

Axis

An imaginary line that the Earth turns on.

Test your learning

On track

1   Jack has drawn a diagram which shows the position of the Sun during the day.

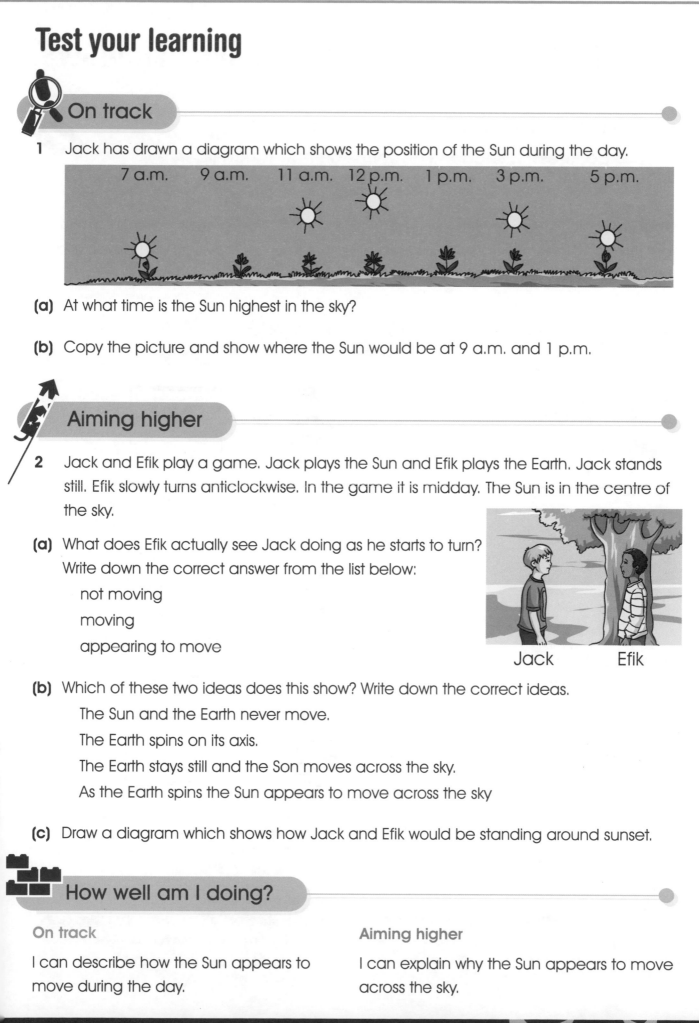

7 a.m.   9 a.m.   11 a.m.   12 p.m.   1 p.m.   3 p.m.   5 p.m.

(a) At what time is the Sun highest in the sky?

(b) Copy the picture and show where the Sun would be at 9 a.m. and 1 p.m.

Aiming higher

2   Jack and Efik play a game. Jack plays the Sun and Efik plays the Earth. Jack stands
    still. Efik slowly turns anticlockwise. In the game it is midday. The Sun is in the centre of
    the sky.

(a) What does Efik actually see Jack doing as he starts to turn?
     Write down the correct answer from the list below:

        not moving

        moving

        appearing to move

Jack   Efik

(b) Which of these two ideas does this show? Write down the correct ideas.

        The Sun and the Earth never move.

        The Earth spins on its axis.

        The Earth stays still and the Son moves across the sky.

        As the Earth spins the Sun appears to move across the sky

(c) Draw a diagram which shows how Jack and Efik would be standing around sunset.

How well am I doing?

On track

I can describe how the Sun appears to
move during the day.

Aiming higher

I can explain why the Sun appears to move
across the sky.

29 Which materials make the best shadows?

- Different materials **block** different amounts of light.
- The darkness of shadows depends on how much light is blocked.

Opaque materials let very little or no light through them. **Translucent** materials let some light through. **Transparent** materials let a lot of light through. They can all make shadows. The more the light is blocked the darker the shadow.

How much light do materials block?

What shadows do these materials make?

Opaque materials like these block all or most of the light which hits them.

Translucent materials like these block most of the light that hits them.

Transparent materials make a very faint shadow.

The shadow of the opaque material is very dark because all the light is blocked.

The shadow of the transparent cotton is semi-dark because all the light isn't blocked.

The shadow of this transparent tracing paper is faint because very little light is blocked.

Opaque

A property of a material which lets no light pass through it.

Transparent

A property of a material which lets light pass through it.

Test your learning

On track

1   Jack has collected a few different materials. He thinks about the shadows they will form.

(a) Sort these materials into those which are opaque, translucent and transparent.

(b) Which two will block the most light?

(c) Draw the shadow each material will make.

Aiming higher

2   In a dark room, Yin and Lucy hold some objects between a lamp and a wall.

They see the plastic toy makes a dark shadow and the tracing paper a faint shadow.

(a) Explain why the shadows are so different.

(b) Name three materials which make faint shadows.

(c) Explain why even transparent materials make shadows.

How well am I doing?

On track	Aiming higher
I can describe the shadows made by different materials.	I can explain why even transparent materials make shadows.

Index